BECOMING ME — A METAMORPHOSIS

BECOMING ME — A METAMORPHOSIS

SHELIA POWELL

SAPPHIRE BOOKS

SALINAS, CALIFORNIA

Becoming Me - A Metamorphosis
Copyright © 2016 by **Shelia Powell**. All rights reserved.

ISBN - 978-1-943353-51-4

This is a work of fiction - names, characters, places, and incidents are the product of the author's imagination or are used fictitiously. Any resemblance to actual persons living or dead, business, events or locales is entirely coincidental.

All rights reserved. No part of this publication may be reproduced, distributed, or transmitted in any form or by any means, including photocopying, recording, or other electronic or mechanical methods, without written permission of the publisher.

Book Designer - LJ Reynolds
Cover Designer - Michelle Brodeur

Sapphire Books Publishing, LLC
P.O. Box 8142
Salinas, CA 93912
www.sapphirebooks.com

Printed in the United States of America
First Edition – October 2016

This and other Sapphire Books titles can be found at
www.sapphirebooks.com

Dedication

To my wife...Always

Acknowledgments

A big thank you to my children who lived through the dark parts of my life and came out on the other side as wonderful adults.

Thank you to everyone who loves me. I hope you won't judge me for not talking a lot about this as I was going through it.

Sapphire Books, thank you so much for giving me this opportunity to birth this baby, which is so raw, gritty and different from my others. You rock!

Thanks to everyone who read the poetry and gave feedback to make it better.

Finally, thanks to my wife who loves and supports me and does my typing (which I hate) sometimes.

I love you all!

Forward

Dear younger self,

I wrote this book to tell you that even though your life was hard, there were some great parts in it as well. The horrible things that occurred were just a small part when compared to the love of your parents, the birth of your children, your friends and finding the love of your life.

I know at times the world seemed difficult, but remember that with good comes bad. I am so very proud that your heart was strong enough to make it through all that you faced. I also hope "Becoming Me" will end up in the hands of the people who need it most.

You did good kid!

Love,
Your older self

Table of Contents

Larva

Childhood Memory	14
Stolen Innocence	15
Little Girl Lost	17
Rest In Peace	18
Are You Dead	19
LOL	20
Orange Slice Cake	21
Life's Little Box	22
The Myth Of Happiness	23
Parents	24
Best Friend	25
Voices	26
Acceptance	27
Because You Live	28
Exposed	30
Duality	32
Self Esteem	**33**

Chrysalis

The Moment I Met You	36
Pain	37
Worst Memory	38
Becoming A Man	39
God's Angel	41
Dreams	43
Frailty	45
Metamorphosis	46
The Tide	48
Integration	49

Words Left Unspoken	51
My Friend	52
Drowning	53
Let Me Be Me	55
Nothing To Give	56
Silence	58
The Raging Storm	60
The Blade	61
Scars	62
The Tempest	63
The Winding Road	64
Cravings	65
Today	66
Why	67
Poison	68
A Sharp World	69
Blue Eyes and Glitter	70
Blood Red Tears	71
Crimson	72
Descent Into Hell	74
Liar	75
Kill Me Softly	76
Soar	77
My Guardian Angel	79
Seasons	81

Butterfly

Hello	85
First Kiss	86
Forever	87
Now	88
Blue Eyes	89
Gentle Reassurance	90

Miles Apart	91
Heart And Soul	92
Together	93
Wounded Doves	94
Suddenly	95
Gently, Lovingly, Forever	96
Linked	97
Sleeping	98
The Gift	99
Music	100
Realization	101
Forever	102
I Want Love	103
Touch Me	105
I Do	106
Daddy	107
The Silent Vow	108
Light Of Day	109
Ode To Momma And Daddy	110
Sent From Above	111
Woman To Woman	112
Why I Love You	114
Infinity	116
Conversations	117
Future	118
Happiness	119
Afterword	120

Photo and Definition courtesy of;

www.wpclipart.com
www.wikipedia.org

LARVA

- *n. pl.* **lar·vae** (-vē) or **lar·vas** : The newly hatched, wingless, often wormlike form of many insects before metamorphosis.

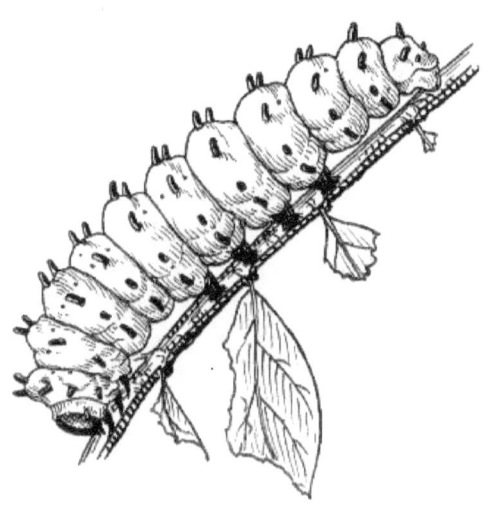

The word *larva* referring to the newly hatched form of insects before they undergo metamorphosis comes from the Latin word *lārva,* meaning "evil spirit, ghost, demon."

In the 17th and 18th centuries, scientists began to use the Latin word to describe the stage in an insect's life during which its final form is still hidden—the larval stage is a mask, so to speak, that the insect will later remove to reveal its adult appearance.

Childhood Memory

In the car
Singing songs about Santa
Content, warm, important
Snowflakes slowly falling

Loved.

Stolen Innocence

Why did you take my innocence?
I was not ready.
I did not wish for it.
I did not ask for it.
Too young to know
That I could just refuse.
Too young to even know
What was happening.
Did you enjoy the power you held
Over me?
Did you realize
The fear you caused?
Did that, too, bring
You pleasure?

Why did you take my innocence?
It was not yours
To take.
It was mine
To give,
When I was ready,
When there was
No fear.
Why did you
Leave me with the
Guilt you should feel?

Did you ever feel
The pain
The guilt
The self-loathing
That you left
With me?
Or did you feel
Only pleasure
From the power
That you held
Over a child?

What gave you
The right
To take my innocence?

Little Girl Lost

When I look into the mirror,
In your haunted, puppy dog eyes,
I feel such profound sadness
For the little girl
That never was.
The one that was
Forced to become a woman
By the monster that knew better but
Took what he wanted anyway.
The one who
Made you into the tortured
Soul
That you are today.
The one that is to blame
Is not you, never you!
I look into your
Haunted, puppy dog
Eyes,
And I weep
For the
Little Girl
Lost.

Rest in Peace

Now that you're dead,
I often wonder if you rest in peace.
How could you~
after all you did to me.

I was only a young child,
you were the adult.
You knew better,
I knew only fear.

Why me, did I do something?
Something that led you to rape my soul
with your touch?
Was it my fault?

Or, would any child have been adequate,
have caused you to do things
that they did not understand
and to instill in them self-hate?

Do you rest in peace?
I hope not,
for I never rest
at all.

Are you Dead

You are dead
Cold, rotting, fleshless bones.
I know that you are no longer
On this earth.
No longer able to
Hurt me.
But you do.
You have hurt me everyday
In my mind
And in my soul.
You with your
Cold, rotting, fleshless bones.
You will never fully
Be dead,
Because your actions
Keep you alive
In me.
Hurting me, torturing me,
Making me feel
So cold
That I wonder,
Are you dead?
Or is the one that
Is truly dead
Me?

LOL

My daddy twirls
Me round and round
The blue sky swirls
I laugh out loud

Orange Slice Cake

My momma pulls out
The orange slice candy and mix for cake
I pull up my chair
It's time to bake
A surprise for Daddy

Life's Little Box

Where do I fit in?
Where would you have me to…
In a neat little cubbyhole that you created,
With all of your expectations met?
I feel like a round peg trying to fit
Into the square hole that you carved for me.
Why do you try to push me into where you want me to go?
Mold me into what you want me to be?
I am not you. I am me.
I am my own person.
I choose who and what I want to be.
I am in control.
So stop trying to fit me into
one of your little boxes!

The Myth of Happiness

Sitting in a crowd,
Smiling, laughing, perpetuating
the myth of happiness.

Knowing nothing of the things
that are happening around you,
feeling nothing but the pain
of emptiness.

A void, a space, a hole,
a place where something should be,
but is not,
a vortex of vast nothingness.

Sitting in a crowd,
Smiling, laughing, perpetuating
The myth of happiness.

Parents

Momma
Gentle, female
Loving, giving, sharing
Beautiful, loyal, tough, fair
Supporting, sharing, loving
Rugged, male
Daddy

Best Friend

My best friend, Carla
There from the beginning
Making me happy
With her raucous, low laughter
I love her dearly

Voices

Can you hear the voices
That are always with me?
If so, what do they say to you?
Do they say,
"Be happy, sad, depressed,
Live, die, love, hate, hurt"
As they do to me?
Should I listen?
Can I help but?
Do you hear them,
Do you listen?
I do.

Acceptance

Why can't you accept me
As I am?
I can be no more, no less
Than who I am.
I try to be who everyone wants
But I am who I am.
I crave love, respect, happiness.
But who really values who I am?
Am I not worthy enough to earn this
Just by being who I am?
Do I not meet expectations of others
Due to who I am?
If I can't please anyone
By being who I am,
Then why bother…
Because I can't change who I am.
So, should I cease living this life
With no one ever knowing who I really was?

Because You Live

Do you feel love?
The sweet tender moments
Of knowing you are the only one
I don't.

Do you feel hate?
Not for yourself, but for others
Or even towards others
I don't.

Do you feel pain?
Not like a toothache
But the kind deep inside your being
I don't.

Do you feel desire?
The kind that is hot, passionate,
The desire I want
I don't.

Do you feel lonely?
The type where everyone leaves,
Just walks away
I don't.

Do you feel excited?
Like a child at Christmas

Opening their first present from Santa.
I don't

Do you feel sad?
Like a child whose puppy
Has been hit by a car.
I don't.

Do you feel happy?
The kind that comes
When you hold a newborn babe.
I don't.

Why do you get to experience feelings of
Love, hate, pain, desire,
Loneliness, excitement, sadness and happiness,
When I simply do not feel at all?

It is simply because you live.

Exposed

Tears flow freely
From my eyes.
I had hoped
That they would
Cleanse me.
Like the water of
A baptismal pool
That washes sin
From others.
Instead they feel
Like the flames
Of hades
Spilling
From my body,
Licking at my face,
Consuming me,
The stench permeating
The air around me
As my skin peels
Away,
Exposing me for what
I really am,
A succubus.
A taker of souls.
A giver of nothing.
My cover now
Sheds.

Tears will never
Cleanse this evil
Soul
That shall ever burn
In my own
Self-imposed
Hell.

Duality

The two sides fight for acceptance
But to the outside only one can win
It's the bubbly over achiever
For, to me, weakness is a sin

Self Esteem

Falling, falling,
down, down, down
Like a leaf in autumn.
Once lush, supple, green, alive.
Then orange, treasured, beautiful.
Now spiraling downward, out of control,
brown, crackling, underfoot,
confused, hurting, lonely,
lifeless, forgotten, dead.

Photo and Definition courtesy of;

www.clipart.com
www.wikipedia.org

CHRYSALIS

(n:) a moth or butterfly at the stage of growth when it is turning into an adult and is enclosed in a hard case.

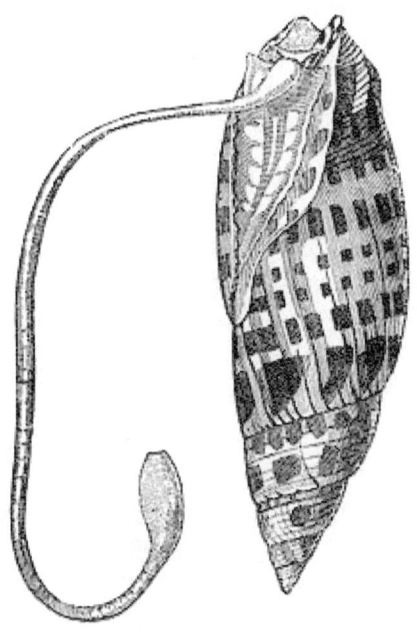

As soon as a larva is done growing and has reached their full length and weight, they form themselves into a chrysalis. From the outside of the pupa, it looks as if the caterpillar may just be resting, but the inside is where all of the action is. Inside of the pupa, the caterpillar is rapidly changing and growing.

The Moment I Met You

What the hell was I thinking
What the hell did I do
By giving my heart freely
The moment I met you.

I was convinced
That this whole thing was right
And I gave myself wholly
Without even a fight.

Love doesn't come easy
I wish that it did
For my whole life I wouldn't have
Kept my heart hid.

Now there is pain
As I knew there would be
And I feel so foolish
Why couldn't I see.

What the hell was I thinking
What the hell did I do
By giving my heart freely
The moment I met you.

Pain

Pain wracks my body
As your words cut my heart.
Your verse spills out
Like invisible darts.

You know which words hurt me,
Which buttons to push,
And you come in stealthily from behind
For your carefully planned ambush.

You must know you hurt me
But do you really care?
Do you do it purposefully,
Or are you unaware?

No, you are aware of the pain
That you cause me,
The anguish that you inflict,
Why can't you let me be?

The pain wracks my body
As your words cut my heart.
Like a knife piercing through me
My soul begins to depart.

Worst Memory

In the bed
Sleeping peacefully
Drowsy, cozy, tranquil
Phone rings...Momma is dead

Anguish!

Becoming a Man

"Mom, I'm in love,
What do I do?"
"Well son I know
Nanny sent her to you."

I never thought
That these words I'd hear
From my quiet, shy child
That I hold so dear.

Always the follower.
So mild and so meek.
But I knew in my heart
That you were not weak.

And then came the day
That your nanny died.
She was your best friend,
The one who you would confide.

I worried so much
About you on that day.
I did not know how you would feel
When she went away.

But you surprised everyone,
Stepped up and took control,

Just like you knew that
This was now your role.

You made us so proud
When you came out of that shell.
You became a man
When all those walls fell.

And then your Nanny
Sent a family to you.
They made you so happy
That you knew what to do.

So when you asked me
On that wonderful day,
I said "Follow your heart son,
Nanny will show you the way."

You did follow your heart,
Now with kids and no strife.
We are all proud and love you,
And of you and your life!

God's Angel

A tiny bundle
Came into my life
On a September eve
With very little strife.

She entered the world
With wide eyes of blue.
A heart so big,
And a spirit that flew.

The more that she grew
So precious and sweet,
A happier child
You would never meet.

She never met a stranger,
She loved everyone.
Bubbly, laughing, and accepting,
To all she was fun.

Now this tiny bundle
Into a beautiful young woman has grown.
And I realize that she is God's Angel,
Down here on loan.

God's Angel from Heaven,
What did I do,

To deserve such a gift
As precious as you?

You are my daughter,
My teacher as well as my friend,
And, we share a love
That will never end.

Each and every day I look up
To thank God for your enchanting hug,
Your kisses, and for your precious love
That you give so freely, my Kelly-Bug.

Dreams

The football star.
State wrestling champ.
Then one summer
at football camp,
"A torn tendon"
Was all they said.
And, with those three words
a dream was dead.
In the heart of a child
the dream began;
but it all ended
in the heart of a man.
The depression expected
just never came,
where it was anticipated,
there flickered a flame.
"Never give up."
He said to me.
"I will be successful,
everyone will see.
Who am I now everyone asks.
Well, I am not defined
by the sports I played
but by my mind.
So watch out world,
step back and see
what the Good Lord

has in store for me.
I may be down,
but I am not out.
Now everyone will know
what I am really about.
I do not give up.
I'll never give in.
No matter what,
I am going to win!"
These words I heard
with tears in my eyes.
How could someone so young
be so wise.
His dreams have shifted.
A new life began,
and I am so proud
to call him my son.

Frailty

Clever, bright, smart
gifted, intellectual, sharp
talented, exceptional, astute.

Foolish, crazy, folly
idiocy, weird, peculiar
eccentric, lunacy, madness.

Such a frail, pathetic filament
between genius and insanity.

Metamorphosis

Perfection
> Stunning, brilliant, superlative,
> Obedient, vigorous, exceptional,
> Respected, admired, courteous,
> Fit, compassionate, successful.

Reality
> Molestation, incest, family secrets,
> Drugs, promiscuity, alcohol,
> Bulimia, lies, shattered dreams
> Hate, damaged existence.

Peer
> Into the looking glass
> Holding it close to your face,
> Seeing what you want
> Others to perceive.

Smile
> At the perfection that everyone
> Outside your realm of self
> Observes you to be,
> Even though you know different.

Gaze
> Deeper in the mirror.
> Become aware of the tears
> Accumulating in the corners
> Of your eyes.

Perceive
> The actuality of the being
> That you truly are,
> No matter what others
> Catch a glimpse of.

Observe
> As the transformation
> Commences taking place,
> And others begin to
> Notice the difference.

Resist
> The fact that perfection
> Is simply a mask worn
> To conceal reality so that
> Love and adoration is assured.

Understand
> That when the mask begins to collapse,
> Exposing all the flaws
> That there is no fight left,
> And exhaustion has set in.

Madness
> Has moved stealthily into existence
> Eating at your soul,
> Winning the fight.
> Metamorphosis is now complete.

The Tide

The ebb and flow of the ocean
As the tide plays around my feet,
Reminds me of my minds work
For never the two halves meet.
One side spirals upward
As the other plunges down,
The ebb and flow of my sanity
Turns my world around.
And, as my world starts spinning
A hurricane starts to build.
Which is the stronger willed?
The side that wants to giggle,
Get angry, shout, or shop,
That really has no boundaries,
And never knowns when to stop.
Or the side that wants to withdraw,
Just sit and stare and cry,
Or maybe try to take my life,
Because all I really want is to die.
Day in, day out, I suffer
With the ebb and flow of the tide.
Searching for an answer,
Or just in someone to confide.
The hurricane now is calming…
The tide is going out…
My mind is quieting down now,
This is what Bipolar is really all about.

Integration

The two halves of my whole
trying to integrate, to become one,
the left side depressed,
the right craving fun

My left brain takes over
And I crash quickly to the ground,
Crawl into my bed to cry,
Hate myself and beat myself down.

Then the right brain jumps in
And transports me to the sky.
I am upbeat, friendly, and talkative
As blissfully I fly.

The dilemma I have with this
Is that I just never know
From hour to hour, day to day,
Which way my emotions will go.

I fly up, I crash down,
I want to live or I crave death,
I love myself extravagantly,
Or yearn to breathe my last breath.

How can I live wholly,
Never knowing which I will be,

Not knowing if mania or depression
Is the REAL me…

I just crave the two halves of my whole
To integrate and be one.
So that I can finally be normal
And my minds battle will be done.

Integration

Words Left Unspoken

As I lay the blade on my thigh
To make the very first cut
I begin to think about why.

The first thing that comes to me uncle dear,
As I make the first cut for you,
Is the pain of the rape at four years old, could you feel my fear?

Gang rape is reason number two.
And I make separate cuts.
Each one stands alone for the four of you.

The fifth and final cut is for me and the words left unspoken.
But saying them now loud and clear,
I know that I may be bleeding, but I am not broken.

My Friend

I have a friend
That will bring me bliss,
And calm my soul
With its razor blade kiss.

The sweetest kisses
That I have known,
Have come from a blade
When I'm all alone.

All alone once more
Without you by my side,
I draw the edge down my arm
Using my veins as a guide.

Veins so blue, blood running so red,
Now calm is settling within.
Thank you for your razor blade kisses,
My one and only friend.

Drowning

Drowning, drowning,
In a sea of beautiful people.
Searching, searching,
For a familiar face,
Realizing that they have no faces,
They are only faceless beings.
Feeling the hands of fate
Reaching out to pull me under.
Looking, looking for a way out.
Seeing nothing but the writhing, roiling bodies
That want to keep me down.
Further and further they pull me under.
As I try to reach up, up,
Away from imminent demise.
They are stronger, stronger,
These unseen faces
As they pull at me.
Wanting me, grasping for me,
Loving me, loathing me,
Pulling me down as I fight,
Wanting to release me, knowing they cannot.
For they have crushed me.
Crushed the very core of my being,
Knowing that I cannot survive
Knowing I have no fight.
They writhe with rage
These beings that are no longer alive.

Pulling, always pulling
Smothering me as further down I go,
Losing all sense of being, of self,
Of my very essence.
Drowning, drowning,
Dying, losing the battle, the will, the want.
Giving in, feeling the chill
As further down I go.
Becoming one of them,
The beautiful, faceless, people.
Calling out to others to join us
In our pit of despair.
Seeing the long line of lost souls
Waiting to go under.
Wanting to tell them to run
Even as I reach out
With the others for them,
Feeling them, pulling them,
Drowning, drowning.

Let me Be

Let me lay here,
Just go away
Like everyone else
Who said they would stay.

It's too late now,
Can't you see?
I've gone too far,
Just let me be.

Oh, the blood from my wrists?
Don't you worry
The flow will stop shortly
Please don't act sorry.

I feel no pain now;
The pills have numbed me
I'm fading quickly from this earth
This is for the best, don't you see.

Let me lay here,
Just go away
Like everyone else
Who said they would stay.

Nothing to Give

Why should I think
I have something to give?
When reality is,
I don't want to live.
Living is for the "chosen ones,"
Not defects like me.
I try to act complete,
But look close and you will see.
You will see all the ugliness
That there is inside.
And no matter the pretense
The repulsiveness, I can't hide.
I seem to ruin everything
That I ever touch,
But needing or wanting
Or loving too hard or too much.
Maybe I should vow
Not to "touch" anymore,
Except for myself
As I cut to the core.
I lift my blade up
And watch it come down.
I feel great relief
That no one's around.
No one to stop me.
No one to care.
I cut a bit deeper

Is this really as deep as I dare?
I yearn to cut deeper,
To end my own life,
While I watch as my blood
Flows over the knife
Then out of the blue,
Though the pain's still inside
And the blood flows so freely,
Some craving subsides.
I continue to exist this time,
Though with still nothing to give.
But who knows, next time,
Maybe I will lose motivation to live.

Silence

Standing still in the sands of time
Feeling the ocean wash over my feet
Knowing that the tide is coming in
Feeling the waves as they start to crash
Harder and harder, closer and closer
Reaching out to me
Calling my name
How I love to feel the cool water
Upon my legs
Standing on the precipice
Knowing that only a thin line
Separates me from life and death
Looking back over my shoulder
Seeing nothing but despair
Hovering on the edge
Hearing the oceans cry for me
Looking forward and seeing beauty
Wanting, needing, craving splendor
Plummeting over the edge
With each step feeling more alive
Even as death grows closer
Loving the sounds of the birds
And the crashing waves
Craving silence from the sounds in my head
The hateful, hopeless sounds
Diving in the ocean
Hearing the sound of nothingness

Feeling the relief
Knowing that death is imminent

Embracing it, loving it, wanting it
Finally, silence, blessed silence.

The Raging Storm

A storm starts to build.
Tears fall like raindrops
On the windowpane
Of my soul.
Why must there be
So much heartache?
Why must the suffering
Go so deep?

The storm rages,
Rages like a monsoon
With no end.
Torrents of fury,
Anguish, torment, despair,
Crash like waves
Against the walls of my heart.
Threatening to batter,
Break, crack, destroy,
The small part of me
That is still living,
Beating, giving, loving.

Still, the storm rages on.

The Blade

Rivers of crimson flowing silently,
Pooling in crevices then spilling over,
Trickling, running, gathering speed.
The streams are becoming larger and deeper,
Flowing ever faster.

As I watch, the beauty overtakes me
Fills me with a calm
That I knew would come.

My face serene, my mind quiet,
Watching the beautiful river
Of blood flowing from my body,
Accepting the fact that I am
Crying silently with a blade.

Scars

The scars shine upon my skin
Like the sun on a lake
They rise up, ripple, and glisten
Oh God, what will it take?

What will it take to make me stop
Hurting myself this way?
Picking up the blade to cut,
To make the pain go away.

The pain that is buried deep below,
Now comes spewing up to the surface
And makes me seek relief again
By making me cut away my sins with very little fuss.

Will I ever be able to erase my failings,
Or are they buried too deep inside?
And, no matter how deep I cut
The wrongs will remain, but the scars I'll never hide.

The scars shine upon my skin
Like the sun on a lake
They rise up, ripple, and glisten
Oh God, what will it take?

The Tempest

The tempest rages inside me
Spinning my life around.
The tempest rages inside me
Oh, the intensity of the sound.
The tempest rages inside me
I feel it through and through.
The tempest rages inside me
Oh God, what do I do?

The tempest rages inside me
I see an hourglass with falling sand.
The tempest rages inside me
The knife is now in my hand.
The tempest rages inside me
Please someone calm the storm.
The tempest rages inside me
The blood is oh so warm.

The tempest rages inside me
My time is drawing near.
The tempest is raging inside me
And now I know no fear.
The tempest is now quieting
Darkness is closing in.
The tempest is now silent
For me it's the end.

The Winding Road

Winding, twisting, turning
These roads that I call life.
Why can't it be easy
To follow the straight path,
Instead of being drawn
This way, then that,
Never knowing what
Is just around the bend,
Searching for love on this journey
But finding only pain.

Cravings

I am supposed to crave
A husband
A career
2.1 children
A white house with a picket fence
And a mini-van in the driveway.

And all I truly crave,
Is the gentle touch
of a woman!

Today

Today I will cut
Today I will bleed
Today I will want
But can't admit that I need.

Today I need
Today I want to feel hope
Today I feel lonely
And unable to cope.

Today I can't cope
Today I can't see
Today I am blind
To the person who is me.

Today I can't see the person who is me
Today I can think of only one deed
Today I will cut
And today I will bleed.

Why?

Why?
Why do I rise up to the sky
Only to plummet back to earth again?

Why?
Why do I feel like a queen
Only to feel like a subject again?

Why?
Why do I laugh and smile
Only to drop to the depths of despair again?

Why?
Why do I feel so loved
Only to feel so unwanted again?

Why?
Why do I feel a burning need to live
Only to crash and crave death again?

Why?
Why do I feel this way
Only because this is my life?

Why?

Poison

Fear
Writhing in my belly
Like snakes in their den
Twisting, turning, crawling, coiling
Striking at will
Turning me into a quivering, quaking, shell of
Myself
Crawling
Up, up my body
Biting as they go
Striking as if to kill me
Releasing me just short of death
Toying with me
Destroying my soul
Releasing
Crawling back down to my belly
Back into their den
Still writhing, coiling, hissing
Knowing that they can strike at any time
Surprising me, terrifying me
Slowly killing the shell that is my soul
Poison.

A Sharp Wall

What a terribly sharp world
That we live in.
There is no wonder
That we get cut.

Whether it be figuratively or literally
We all suffer from the wounds.
The cuts by pain, cuts by others, cuts by words.
Or, in the worst possible scenario,
Cuts by ourselves.
Some choose to figuratively cut others with harsh words.
Others simply cut themselves to relieve the pain

Why can't we stop the
Harshness of this world?
Because only then
Will we stop cutting ourselves…

Literally.

Blue Eyes and Glitter

Behind the glitter and the glitz
And beautiful blue eyes
Lies animosity and hate
And oh, so many lies.

Deceit, infidelity, and dishonor,
Greed, lust, and drink,
Her cold heart laughs it off
With a sexy laugh and a wink.

She is a user of women,
And she climbs the ladder
Of money, fortune, and fame
And to her indifferent soul, it doesn't matter.

The damage she inflicts
She throws by the way
For she lives her life
Minute by minute, day by day.

Moving on up, stepping on others on the way
The blue eyes and glitter
Hide the lies and duplicity
What a repulsive beauty to be so bitter.

Blood Red Tears

Leave me alone
Let me be
I have to cut
Can't you see

The pain I feel
Is not from the knife
The hurt for me
Is simply from life

Leave me alone
Let me be
I have to cut
Can't you see

Life to you
May seem so great
But to my tortured soul
The blade is my fate

Leave me alone
Let me be
I HAD to cut
Can't you see

The blood red tears flow

Crimson Tears

The tears flow
Down my face
For the child
That I once was.
The innocent child
Who believed
That grown-ups were always
Right.
That you should always do
What they said,
Even though it felt
Wrong,
Even though it
Hurt,
Even though it made me
Feel dirty.
The tears flow
Down my face
For the adult that
I now am.
The grown-up who knows
What is right,
The one that still feels that
It was my fault,
That still feels
Wrong, hurt, and dirty.
The tears flow

Down my face,
Because I see what I have
Become…
Guilty, wrong, dirty,
Ashamed, hurt.
The tears flow
Down my face,
As I look at the blade
In my hand.
The cutting edge
That will release
The horrible feelings,
The feelings of guilt,
Shame and unworthiness.
The tears flow
Down my face,
As I draw the blade
Across my thigh,
Releasing the pain,
The shame, the hurt,
Of the loss of my
Innocence.
The tears now flow
Down my legs,
And they are running
Crimson
Relief from the pain is now mine
For a while…

Descent Into Hell

As I lay on my bed to sleep.
Tears of sorrow run down my cheeks.
The one I care for has gone away.
And my entire life has turned to gray.

Gray as dark, dark as night.
I have no strength left to fight.
When I felt your love I became scared.
And I ran away from the one who cared.

So, here I lie with my tears flowing.
The fear inside me now is growing.
As I descend into the pits of Hell.
For I know that for hurting you, here I will dwell.

Liar

Why do you lie?
Sitting there smugly thinking I believe,
Thinking I don't know who you are,
What you are.
But I do, I know you.
I know what you want, what you need,
And you take this from me.
You take from me because you can,
Because you know that I love you.
But you are only using me
For your own pleasure, your own needs.

But what about me, my needs, my wants,
They mean nothing to you.
For you love only yourself.
You look at me with your empty eyes
And tell me you love me
After you have taken your pleasure.
But I know you, I do,
Why do you lie?

Kill me Softly

"You are so stupid,
You do nothing right."
I heard these words daily,
And no longer fight.

Why can't you understand,
What in the hell can I do?
To make you see the problem
Comes not from me, but from you.

You say, "You are less than I wanted,
More trouble than I thought.
God what was I doing
When it was YOU that I sought."

But in my heart, I know what it was,
Head cheerleader, prom queen,
I was your trophy.
God that was so mean.

I gave you my heart,
My soul and my love,
And you are killing me softly,
This meek, gentle dove.

Go Forth and Soar

I just tried to please you
I truly tried
But at the end of the day
We both lay down and cried.

I put myself out there
By exposing my all
I really thought
That this could be for the long haul.

But I don't know how
Or even if I can take
Not knowing where you are
When you sleep, when you wake.

I understand you hurt
But I am hurting too
And never would I want
To make things worse for you

Trust is so hard
But what can we do
This is bred inside us
So it is not anything new.

I do not want to smother
Be possessive or weak

When a kind word from you
Is all that I seek.

My mind conjures up
The pain from the past
And I know that for me
Love cannot last.

I want too much
And I need even more
So I am releasing you now
Go forth and soar.

Ascend to the mountains
Fly to the sea
You are much better off
Without someone like me

Me that is needy, torn
Shattered, broken and blue
But please know deep in your soul
I will always love you.

But loving for me
Means not making you cry
Just letting you move forward
With a loving goodbye.

So my beautiful friend
Dry your tears, cry no more
Be all you can and
Go forth now and soar!

My Guardian Angel

As I stand upon the bridge
Contemplating my fate,
Should I jump or just walk away
My soul filled with self-hate.

What have I done to bring such heartache my way?
Molestation, bulimia, even rape,
Lies, deception, loathing, failure.
Is this my only escape?

I lift my leg over the railing,
The relief I feel is great.
I have finally found my way out,
I know this is my fate.

My heart is pounding intensely,
My mind is rushing fast.
I know my life on this earth
Is over, never here to last.

As I lean forward over the edge,
And I think of my last breath
I feel adrenaline rushing
As I think of this, my death.

Then all of a sudden
I feel a giant hand on me

I fight, I struggle, I scream,
But he just will not let me be.

I realize this is my Guardian Angel,
Stephen is his name.
And, in this great time of need,
My saving angel came.

He pushed me back to safety,
And said boldly, "you have so much to give,
So your life is not complete.
Go forth child be happy; it is time to live!"

Seasons

How can you be lonely?
You are always surrounded
by those who love you most.

They have their own lives now though
that do not always include you.
This is the natural order of things.

Just as the leaves turn in autumn,
so do our children,
but they turn again in the spring
of their lives.
So that we may enjoy the winter
Of your lives together,

Loneliness will vanish
into the long days of summer
and with it
a rebirth of family

Photo and Definition courtesy of;

www.clipartbest.com
www.wikipedia.org

BUTTERFLY

(n:) butterfly; *(plural noun:)* butterflies
An insect with two pairs of large wings that are covered with tiny scales, usually brightly colored, and typically held erect when at rest. Butterflies fly by day, have clubbed or dilated antennae, and usually feed on nectar.

When the caterpillar has done all of its forming and changing inside the pupa, an adult butterfly emerges. When the butterfly first emerges from the chrysalis, both of the wings are going to be soft and folded against its body. This is because the butterfly had to fit all its new parts inside of the pupa.

As soon as the butterfly has rested after coming out of the chrysalis, it will pump blood into the wings in order to get them working and flapping – then they get to fly. Usually within a three or four-hour period, the butterfly will master flying and will search for a mate in order to reproduce.

When in the fourth and final stage of their lives, adult butterflies are constantly on the look out to reproduce and when a female lays their eggs on some leaves, the butterfly life cycle will start all over.

Hello

How did you
Find me?

Where have
You been?

It was meant
To be.

First Kiss

You put your mouth on mine
And I forgot to breathe.

Forever

You reach out to me, befriend me,
I reach back lovingly, longingly
For I need, want, crave a friend.
A friend who listens, understands
One who is filled with compassion.
Knowing that even though I long for more,
That for now, in this place, in this time
That is all we have.
I am appreciating this wonderful gift
While praying that someday, someway
As we reach towards each other
With the truth of our being;
Beyond now, in another place
We will find love while remaining friends
Forever.

Now

She is like us
Hiding away
In sorrows
Unless
Someone
Cares enough about her
Being in now

I'm calling you out
I know the darkness.
You saved me
Let me
Care about you now
In our
Now.

Blue Eyes

Blue eyes staring at me
From across the room
Love at first sight.

Gentle Reassurance

There are times we have laughed,
Times we have doubted and cried.
But, there is no one but you
That I want by my side.

You, who is "hardened,"
Or so you say,
Have stolen my heart
And took my fears away.

The fears have shadowed me
For much of my life,
That I deserved nothing other than
Lies, hurt, anguish and strife.

But, with your gentle reassurance,
And tender sweet care…
You made me believe I deserve better.
You're the answer to my prayer!

Miles Apart

I can rest
peacefully
knowing
someone
cares.
She sleeps
tranquilly
by my side,
next to me.
Even though
miles apart,
tonight she sleeps
by my side
sharing
pillows and
comfort.

Heart and Soul

I searched for most of my life
And finally
You were there
You touched my heart
And my soul
Was conclusively complete.

Together

I hope that
in now
you are feeling
loved
and wanted
and knowing
that the
darkness cannot
touch you,
me, us,
any longer.
The sunshine
and light
have come into
our hearts
and souls
as together
we become
one...
Forever.

Wounded Doves

When at last I heard your voice
my heart began to pound.
My knees went weak like a new born babe;
I knew that finally love I had found!

I no longer thought it was a dream,
deep in my soul I knew,
that the love I prayed for longingly
was in the voice, the gentle laugh, of you.

You who said that you were broken,
that you thought you had no emotion,
have decided I am worth giving
of your love and devotion.

Now I can start to believe
that in my heart so broken and maimed,
there must be some good in me
if your loving heart I have claimed.

So here we are together like two wounded doves
with hearts that need to mend.
We've started on the path of love
that will never know an end.

Suddenly

Without knowing
How or when or where
Suddenly I felt love
And it was you there.

Gently, Lovingly, Forever

I know that
Here and now
Your love
Is freely flowing
Into my heart
Gently
Lovingly
Forever

My heart responds
By running over
My cup, it overflows
As I return
The beauty given
Gently
Lovingly
Forever

Linked

Hold me ever so gently.
Kiss me ever so sweet.
Make love to me with a passion
That fills us both with heat.

Give to me your heart.
Take from me my love.
For we are linked together
The Dragon and the Dove.

Sleeping

I listen
I hear
I love
The sound
Of you sleeping
By my side

I reach out
To touch your hair
You gently moan
I listen
I hear
I love

The Gift

I have a gift
that is very precious to me.
I am giving it to you now;
Please handle it carefully.

The gift is very fragile
and can so easily break;
that I ask from you a favor,
Good care of it please take.

Nurture it and protect it;
give it the love it needs.
Honor this gift daily
through words as well as deeds.

I ask that you keep it always
and from it never depart.
For I love you baby,
And I give to you my heart!

Music

I listen to a lot of music
And the most beautiful parts
Bring me closer to you.

Realization

My heart is all aflutter,
Beating oh so fast.
I just can't sort these feelings.
Are they present or are they past?

Confusion reigns completely,
Taking over my brain.
Am I coming or am I going,
Is this pleasure or is it pain?

"Love" you say, "that's what this is."
And my mind begins to clear,
As I realize that this is love
And with you, I have nothing to fear.

Forever

You said
"I will love you
Forever if you let me"

I let you.

I Want Love

I want to be loved.
I need to feel love.
I want love.

Not the feeling of new love
When everything is exciting and fresh
And every touch sets you on fire.

But the kind of love
That has been tried and tested
By the tides of time.

Not the love in which the
Heat of passion must be
Alleviated each time you are together.

But the love that is felt
When you are reached for in the middle of the night
Simply because you are there.

Not the love of selfishness,
Vanity, duty, or
Simply put convenience.

But the love of respect, triumphs,
Shared memories and even tragedies
Past and present.

I want to be loved,
I need to be loved,
I want love.

And I have found it…
With you.

Touch me

You touched me gently
I responded with a sigh
Happiness was mine

I Do

When on the plane we stepped
To fly off to start a new life
Excitement bubbled over
For on this trip I would become your wife

I was exponentially excited
To step into this role
For I loved you completely
With all my heart and soul

You who had shown me
What I had known all along
That my heart was to be given
To a woman whose love for me was strong

Strong enough that when
I betrothed to you my heart
I hold on to the knowledge
That we would never part

Finally, when the clergy
Underneath the suns enveloping rays
Smiled and pronounce us married
I knew it was forever and always

Daddy

Maybe I was wrong on the day you went
to Heaven
Your life was not over, it had
just begun.
So now I am learning that my life has
not diminished.
Like you, I am beginning, neither of us
is finished.
So, Daddy, let's move forward; neither life ended
this day
We just have to live, learn, and love in a
different way.
I love you so much Daddy, so now
let's live
Because to the world, we still have so much
To give.

The Silent Vow

As the sun peeks above the ocean
A fullness fills my heart;
Along with it the knowledge
That from her I'll never part

I watch her as she's sleeping,
And know I'm truly blessed.
And as she sighs so sweetly,
Quietly, my love to her I profess.

I enjoy the morning stillness
Listening to her sounds;
Hoping her love, like mine,
Simply knows no bounds.

A silent vow I make to her
As she starts to wake;
That I will love and cherish her
Until my dying breath I take.

Light of Day

As we walked along the shoreline,
Beneath the deep blue sky
Side by side together
I felt like I would cry.

Cry tears for the time wasted
For all the time I lied
And for all the years
My truth I had to hide.

Now I have stepped out
Into the light of day
My heart no longer hidden
Under the Suns bright rays

I know I am complete now
As we continue along the sand
And you, my wife, reach quietly
To gently take my hand.

Ode to Momma and Daddy

As I gaze up toward heaven
I can feel a gentle breeze
As it caresses my face
With a gentle touch
The way you used to do

I lift my arms up also
To savor the peaceful sensations
The light wind feels so soothing
As it wraps me in its embrace
The way you used to do

I breathe the air in deeply
And smell the fragrant bouquet
Of fresh cut flowers, sunshine, and love,
The aroma surrounds me completely
The way you used to do

I call out to say "I love you"
For I feel that you are near,
Then I hear your voice on the wind
Whispering "I love you too"
The way you used to do
Caress
Embrace
Aroma
Love
You still do

Sent from Above

She lay her head gently
Upon my chest
And snuggles closely
To suckle my breasts.

This woman I love
With my whole heart
Knows how to ready me
My legs fall apart.

Her body moves downward,
Her tongue touches my clit
The wetness grows creamier
As she nibbles just a bit.

I gasp at the contact,
Raise my hips to her mouth
This was the love I craved
With her there is no doubt.

My body, it trembles
I cry out as I came
Every bit of my insides
Are licked by the flame

I have waited so long
For a woman to love
And she has been sent
To me from above.

Woman to Woman

Woman to woman
Skin to skin
Our flesh ignites
Again and again

A single touch
Is all it takes
From you my love
To make my body quake

My body ready
Your hand slips inside
The heat boils over
As hearts collide

With each loving thrust
You gaze into my eyes,
Whisper that you love me
Our temperatures rise.

You flip me over
On you I know ride
Sweating and naked
Nothing to hide

Our pace increases
Our bodies so wet

I plead with you
As deeper you get

With one final push
I let out a scream
And cover us both
With natures cream

Your eyes glint as you look up and say
"Baby, can I have more?"
I simply smile gently
And reply "Honey, I'm yours!"

Why I Love You

You ask me why I love you;
I give much thought to this.
One of the reasons I think of
Is that you bring me happiness.

Even when I'm angry,
You find a way to make me smile.
You give my life meaning.
You make it all worthwhile.

You tell me that I'm beautiful
Even when I don't feel that way.
You give me your sweet kisses
At the end of every day.

When I'm lonely, scared or sad;
You hold me to your breast
And fill me with such comfort
That I can finally rest.

You watch my sappy TV shows,
And you don't laugh at me when I cry.
You simply get the Kleenex
So that I can dry my eyes.

When I am having a bad day,
You try to understand.

You sit on the couch beside me,
And simply hold my hand.

You give to me so freely
Expecting nothing in return.
You call me just to check on me
And always show concern.

The way you love our "babies"
Even when so bad they've been,
Fills me with emotion
And I love you all over again.

You make love to me so beautifully,
Then look at me with eyes of blue
And whisper that you love me;
This I know is true.

You ask me why I love you
I truly thought you knew,
The reason that I love you
Is just because you're you!

Infinity

While you are sleeping,
let your dreams
come into being.
Dream of me
often as
I dream of
you.
Love me
always
as I shall love you.
In the now,
in the future,
for infinity.

Conversations

Do you
Remember our private
Conversations
When you said?

Remember me
When I said?
Don't you dare
Give up on us now.

Future

I don't know where
We'll go
Or
What we'll see
Just as long
As
You are with me

Happiness

So warm is the sun
As it beats
Down on the
Trees that hold
The larva.

Wings start to
Grow and flutter
As the chrysalis
Struggles to
Break free.

Finally, the beautiful
Butterfly emerges from
It's tough covering
As it comes to life
And flies!

Happiness

Afterword

Dear Reader,
I hope you found this book at the exact time you needed it.
The time you wanted:
To cut
To commit suicide
To give up on finding yourself
Or finding love

You are not alone, I lived this life and, at the exact time you need it,
You won't cut
Or commit suicide
And you will find yourself
And love
Just as I did.
Love,
Shelia

About the Author

The first psychic-medium ever used on The Travel Channel's Ghost Adventures, Shelia is known for her special blend of homespun humor and gentle compassion. She has a large client base spanning several countries. Among her clients are people from all walks of life including physicians, lawyers, other psychic mediums, teachers, business owners, professional athletes, award winning authors, and soccer moms.

Shelia also has an ever-growing celebrity base which includes stars of Baywatch and Ghosts of Girlfriends Past, as well as cast and/or crew of House, Entourage, Brothers and Sisters, CSI Miami, Melrose Place 2009, 90210, Star Trek (2009, 2010), We Are Men, Mad Men, Dallas, and Masters of Sex, to name a few.

Shelia is a Certified Spiritual Coach, Intuitive, Empath, Medium, ULC Minister, and Reiki Master.

Shelia has been writing her whole life but finally published her first book, Memoirs Of The Happy Lesbian Housewife, in October 2014 under the nom de plume of Lorraine Howell. It was a finalist for a Goldie Award. The stretch into paranormal books was a natural and necessary progression.

Contact Info:
Website: sheliapowell.com
Email: sheliapowellauthor@gmail.com
Facebook: facebook.com/sheliapowellauthor
Twitter: twitter.com/SheliaP_Psychic

Other books by Shelia Powell

Memoirs of the Happy Lesbian Housewife: You Can't Make This Stuff up Seriously! - ISBN - 978-1-939062-69-7

"A heartwarming reflection written with humor, wit and just the right amount of sarcasm, Lorraine Howell's fun and conversational style reels you in. Sit back and laugh as she shares what makes her "The Happy Lesbian Housewife." Jennie McNulty, Comedian, Co-host of LA Talk Radio show "Cathy is In, The Cathy DeBuono Show" and author of a weekly(ish) blog on Lesbian.com. With a partner named Sweetie, three grown children that are threatening to go into the witness protection program and a career as an adult entertainer, Lorraine Howell delivers a somber, no nonsense look at the difficulty of coming out late in life and how it has affected her poor, pitiful family... NOT! She really brings you a weight-loss book that guarantees that by simply reading her tome word for word, you will lose 25 pounds by the end. HA! Don't you wish? "Memoirs Of A Happy Lesbian Housewife - You Can't Make This Stuff Up. Seriously!" is truly a no-holds-barred, irreverent collection of stories looking at the late-blooming lesbian, Howell, and her hilarious take on life, love, friends, family and SEX! Nothing is off limits...Did we mention SEX? So hop on board and enjoy the ride. You will laugh and cry then laugh some more. Lorraine Howell's The Happy Lesbian Housewife, will not disappoint!

Finding Home – ISBN – 978-1-943353-04-0

Firestarter Kayla Cruise has been kicked out of another foster home, her twelfth, and she's back at the railroad tracks where she always finds solace. Surprisingly, a woman shows up there as an apparition, offering something Kayla had been longing for all her life, a forever home. Not just any home, Tia Keating runs a group home for teens with special gifts, gifts like the ones Kayla has spent years running from.

The problem is that when something feels like it is too good to be true, it usually is. Evil is stalking Kayla and her new family. The Darkness is putting her dream placement in jeopardy. It also threatens a burgeoning relationship that Kayla doesn't quite understand, as well as the only true family she has ever known.

With the help of Tia and the rest of the family, Kayla is going to fight back. The demons won't get to take away her happiness, not this time. Will this placement be her Lucky Thirteen or will The Darkness destroy Kayla's hope for a happily ever after?

www.ingramcontent.com/pod-product-compliance
Lightning Source LLC
Chambersburg PA
CBHW021442080526
44588CB00009B/649